MAKE THE MOST OF IT

LEAVING A LEGACY THAT WILL LAST AFTER LIFE IS OVER

Richard C. Smith

Copyright © by Richard C. Smith 2022. All rights reserved.

Before this document is duplicated or reproduced in any manner, the publisher's consent must be gained. Therefore, the contents within can neither be stored electronically, transferred, nor kept in a database. Neither in Part nor full can the document be copied, scanned, faxed, or retained without approval from the publisher or creator.

TABLE OF CONTENTS

INTRODUCTION 4

CHAPTER 1 9
OWN YOUR STORY 9

CHAPTER 2 28
TRACKING DOWN SATISFACTION 28

CHAPTER 3 50
LAY OUT YOUR LIFE MISSION 50

CHAPTER 4 71
BALANCE BETWEEN WORK AND LIFE ACTIVITIES............71

CHAPTER 5 86
CREATE ENERGY TO ACHIEVE YOUR GOALS 86

CHAPTER 6 92
PICK APART YOUR LIFE 92

CHAPTER 7 109
TRANSFORMING OBLITERATION INTO A VALUABLE OPEN DOOR 109

CHAPTER 8 119
INFLUENCE LEADERSHIP TO ACHIEVE ANYTHING 119

CONCLUSION 133

INTRODUCTION

As you age, leaving a heritage might turn out to be progressively significant. It's consoling to realize that after you're gone, a piece of you will remain. Your loved ones will always remember you; however, "heritage" goes past memories.

Imagine a scenario where you need to establish a long-term impression that is more widespread. There's more than one method for leaving a heritage. This guide will assist you with understanding what leaving a heritage implies, as well as what you can do to ensure you're remembered.

What is a Heritage?

What does it mean to leave a heritage? Consider individuals you've found out about yet never met. Your great-great-grandparents, for example, or a famous person who passed on hundreds of years before you were born.

Leaving a heritage implies having an effect that will keep going long after you pass on. It very well may be monetary, with something you create, or through the people you touched while you were alive. The uplifting news is it's never past time to begin dealing with building a heritage that will outlast you.

How to Leave a Heritage

Okay, so you might say, "I would rather not leave a heritage." There's nothing wrong with that. However, before you dismiss it altogether, take a gander at the different ways you can leave a heritage. You might observe that your focus is restricted to your own kids and grandkids, or you might like to have a touching funeral that allows everybody an opportunity to bid farewell. Here are ways to leave a lasting heritage, both small and large scale

Assess Your Life

All things considered, leaving a heritage is basically realizing that you've left your mark on the world. The best thing to do is stop where you are currently and assess.

On the off chance that you kicked the bucket today, what might individuals say regarding you? Could it be said that you are content with being known for that?

In the event that you don't like what you find, you can begin requesting how to leave a heritage that would satisfy you. Record what you'd like for individuals to say regarding you and begin carrying on with a day-to-day existence that will get that going.

Pass Along Your Qualities

For some, the leaving a heritage definition applies explicitly to the future. In the event that you have children, investigate the model you're setting for them. Have you imparted the qualities you hold dear to them, both through example and by educating them?

Regardless of whether you have children or not, you can in any case pass your qualities to younger generations. You don't need to stroll around asking outsiders, "Could I at any point be your heritage?" Instead, consider volunteering to assist with a youth group or mentor youth sports. There's no restriction on the chances to have an effect on people in the future.

Practice Generosity

While you're taking a gander at leaving a heritage model, you'll most likely see a typical topic. Generous people will generally touch more lives and, therefore, leave a more grounded heritage. You've presumably seen that if you've attended funerals. Words like "giving spirit," "always cared about others," and "huge heart" are pretty standard in tributes.

Liberality is genuinely straightforward. You put others first. You get things done to help those out of luck. It very well may be pretty much as basic as assisting a companion who has run into some bad luck or as huge scope as contributing to help after a nearby catastrophe. Assuming it's about family heritage importance, get family individuals on your liberal acts.

Remember, there are no guarantees. Aim to make the most of your life.

1. Live life in such a way that will guarantee you will be remembered warmheartedly when you are no more.
2. Even on the off chance that we carry on with a long, full life, we still all have a termination date sooner or later.
3. Legacy is the effect your life will make on others after you are no more.
4. Create an urge to get going in your life by characterizing your non-negotiables and being purposeful in your day-to-day existence.

CHAPTER 1

OWN YOUR STORY

The story you tell yourself will shape what your identity is and who you become, particularly during tough situations and troublesome changes.

I love a decent story. I likewise love to recount a decent story. As a matter of fact, I assume I'm a very decent narrator!

How do I have any idea about this? Well, I recount to myself these mind-boggling stories constantly!

Goodness, you thought I implied a made-up story? That's right! That is the precise exact thing I'm discussing! Furthermore, it's not because I am a writer, it is far beyond that!

The narratives I mean, in any case, are not kids' accounts - assuming that is the thing you were thinking. They are, as a matter of fact, tales about things I made presumptions about when I was exceptionally youthful.

However, I have some uplifting news for you! You are likewise an extraordinary narrator!

Indeed. We as a whole have tales about why things are how they are a major part of our life. We could call them a conviction. One way or the other, most grown-ups have stories or convictions that are restricting and that keep them down or disrupt everything.

Allow me to give you a model!

I'm constantly down and out. My folks didn't cherish me enough. My craft isn't adequate. I can't make companions. I need more abilities to experience my fantasy. I'm not sufficiently brilliant to accomplish something else. I'm not truly adept at being coordinated. I was never any great at maths. I'm excessively old. I'm excessively youthful. All my adoration must be acquired. My thought process doesn't make any difference. I'm not prepared. I need more time. I won't ever find success. Assuming that I get excessively cheerful or excessively fruitful, I'll curse myself. I'm bad with cash. I'm not self-restrained. I wasn't naturally introduced to the right sort of family. My plate is too full as of now. I need more energy.

Does any of those impact you?

When you have your story and a conviction about something, your psyche searches for things in your day-to-day existence - minutes, encounters, and so on to affirm those convictions, regardless of whether the conviction isn't serving you.

We accept our story is valid. We assemble the proof from our general surroundings. The proof we need to affirm our story, all the time dismissing and overlooking any data or impacts that could punch holes in it. We are not objective with regards to the accounts we educate ourselves concerning the explanation life is how it is and afterward, we stall out and circumvent around and around.

The greatest effect on the human way of behaving is the story we let ourselves know in our minds. Assuming that you change your story you influence your reality.

Give up and claim your story. Possessing our story can be something hard to do. In any case, it is far more worrying and utilizes significantly more energy to go through our entire time on earth running from the story we don't actually care about. Figuring out how to embrace the weaknesses we have is a gamble yet in the event that we don't, we pass up affection, having a place, and euphoria. These are the most significant pieces of our encounters. Just when we are sufficiently courageous to investigate the obscurity will we find the boundless force of our light. Quit struggling. Surrender. You don't need to calm the brain to change your story. You should simply tune in, recognize and afterward let the old story go. Supposing we own the story, we can compose the consummation.

You can't change your past. We can gain from it however and change our future. At the point when you withdraw from the account of your life, the current realities of your past never again decide or restrict what is feasible for the present. You get to pick what your new story will be and you get to alter it as frequently as the need might arise. There are such countless grown-ups that are caught before, clutching a story in view of involvement from 15, 20, or a long time back. You are not what have been going on with you. You are what you decide to turn into. You can decide to utilize the experience to learn and develop as opposed to making it your story.

Push the correct way. We believe assuming we push sufficiently against the things we don't need in life that they will disappear. In all actuality, anything you focus completely on expands. So the harder you push against what you don't need, the more energy it makes inside you about it and the doubtful it is to really disappear. So why not pick something you really need and focus on that instead?

We cannot mend what we don't uncover. It is a piece of an expression, "Name it to Tame it". In the event that we initially don't recognize the aggravation of our story, we can't transform it. On the off chance that we feel disgrace around our story, we really want to name it. Disgrace could do without being named. It flourishes with mystery, and judgment. Whenever it has been named, however, it no longer has a day-to-day existence. We kill it with sympathy, empathy, and love. Anything that your story is, supposing you overlook it or deny it, will characterize you. On the chance that you own it, you get to compose a daring, delightful new completion.

Cherishing yourself through the most common way of claiming your story is the boldest thing you will at any point do. The tales we tell ourselves, in a real sense make up our reality. To impact your reality, you really want to change your story however you should make sure to be cherishing and pardoning yourself. Change is continuously difficult. It tends to be difficult and somewhat muddled. Be good with that. Try not to invest energy thrashing yourself since you had this conviction that life was a sure way and you presently understand that it very well may be unique. Say thank you to yourself for perceiving your old conviction and for the reason it served in showing you the illustration you wanted.

Reality. You either stroll inside your story or own it or you stand beyond your story and hustle for your value. My conviction is that we are innately deserving of a sublime life, so the time has come to possess the narratives and convictions we have been telling ourselves. All that we know or view as evident are simply stories. We track down the truth in them. No matter what section you are in right now, you get to track down reality in your own story on the off chance that you need to. The time has come to relinquish the constraints and associate with the genuine story and watch how all that in your life-altering events.

The Leap Forward

To change a conviction or a story, we need to initially recognize the old story. Pick one aspect of your life where you believe you are keeping down and not giving everything to it. I would urge you to record it on paper. Compose a rundown of what you hold to be true with respect to yourself concerning that region. Model: Cash is...., Getting fit/sound is...., Taking care of oneself is...., Going after another position is...

Then contemplate some of these inquiries and compose your reactions to them and see what streams out.

- What is having this conviction or story setting me back?
- Is this an example I have seen before in different parts of my life?
- What is the reality/the genuine story?
- What might you do any other way assuming that you had no trepidation around this?
- What are you trying not to keep this story?
- What might your new story at any point be?
- What do you need to do another way to help your new certain story/conviction?

A Forerunner Really Taking Shape

Growing up, Howard's dad struggled to accommodate his loved ones. At a certain point, his dad lost his employment because of a physical issue and became jobless. The whole family endured.

While pondering his life, Howard shares how there were a period he disliked his dad for being a disappointment. This apprehension about the disappointment that he connected with his dad drove him to accomplishment.

There was a point, after his dad's passing, that he reevaluated the disdain. He started recognizing that a lot of his prosperity came from his life as a youngster encountering the great and the terrible.

Rather than seeing the side of his dad, which was a "disappointment", he decided to see his dad as a genuine, fair, and serious man that became involved with an unfavorable system.

By rethinking his story, he had the option to move beyond his disdain and start making his motivation. His objective was to make an organization that lined up with his qualities. An organization that had the best medical advantages, wages, and working circumstances for its representatives. He needed to give others what his dad never had.

Howard Schultz, the pioneer behind Starbucks, involved his story in a method for characterizing his motivation, values, and life. He took his past and involved it for good. It formed him into a high-influence legitimate pioneer.

Your Story Shapes Your Identity

What kind of story would you say to yourself? How should it be influencing your way of living?

Envision in the event that Howard would have remained angry with his father and the difficulties it made in their lives. He might have made material progress, yet without the significance and satisfaction of seeking after his qualities.

At the point when we figure out how to acknowledge our story and use it to shape our future, we track down a bona fide way to deal with life and administration.

The narrative of your life isn't your life. It is your story. You are the essayist of that story. It shapes how you view the world and your motivation.

You know, it is the manner by which you grasp yourself through your story that is important, not current realities of your life."

Compose Your Story

As you take a gander at your life what might be the parts? What have been the achievements up to this point that has formed what your identity is?

Exercise: Take a pen and paper. Mark the base left of the page "birth" and in the upper right state "present day". Presently if you somehow happened to expound on your life, what might be the sections? Mark them down here.

By noticing these sections, you could see where your qualities, fears, and convictions come from.

You might see subjects to how you answer affliction. A few serve you and some don't.

What were the minutes in your day-to-day existence where you felt reason and satisfaction? When were you the most stimulated?

These minutes demonstrate your qualities. They mean something to you. Focus and connect with these qualities more consistently.

I have frequently felt that the most ideal way to characterize a man's personality is to search out the specific mental or moral demeanor in which... he felt most profoundly and strongly dynamic and alive. At such minutes there is a voice inside that talks and says: "This is the genuine me!"

Rethink Your Story

Our past doesn't direct our future. It does, notwithstanding, shape us.

Ponder your past and reexamine it into a story that serves the individual you want to be.

Keep in mind; you are the one composing your story. Each extraordinary story has strain. The principal character frequently begins in a single amazing wreck. In any case, that makes the story so amazing!

We watch the change of the long shot and witness how they utilize their story to have an effect on the planet. Make that be you and take the legend's excursion.

What is the story you are telling yourself? How is it that you could claim it, rather than allow it to possess you?

The Force of Possessing Your Story

I truly believe you should realize that you have a groundbreaking story, and it can mend and move others, in light of the fact that possessing your story has power. It is extremely normal to conceal our pasts, push encounters away from view, imagine we're carrying on with an ideal life and take cover behind veils. We live in a culture where we're continually contrasting ourselves with others through online entertainment, so being glad for our accounts, our excursion, and what our identity is has become progressively hard.

We as a whole have portions of our story that are somewhat more challenging to take ownership of than others and that is fine. What I believe you should detract from this is that you have a story. Generally, I hear a ton of companions and peeps locally saying that they have no story, or that their accounts aren't extraordinary or groundbreaking in any capacity.

So those are two things that burden our accounts, the way that you might think it isn't "exceptional" enough, and how we will generally stow away the "terrible" portions of our excursion. All around let me let you know something, there are no terrible encounters that do not merit sharing and every single story is one of a kind, extraordinary and magical.

Why Your Story Matters

I love sharing my own accounts. It causes me to feel powerless, however, I realize that somebody in some place will understand it and associate with me, and I believe that is lovely. My expectation by sharing my story is I might have the option to help somebody, to cause them to feel less alone, and less weird, and assist them with mending.

There's an explanation why individuals are attracted to motion pictures, comics, books, and perhaps of the loveliest expression on earth: once upon a time. We love stories. We ache for them since it's the manner by which we learn. We read different articles on various sites, scouring the web to track down associations, answers for issues, and local areas. By perusing another person's words, contemplations and stories we track down solace. Your story matters since it has the ability to help other people and you.

You Have a Groundbreaking Story

That is correct, you do. No uncertainties, buts, or coconuts. You absolutely have one buddy. And your story mustn't have an outrageous grievance to have a significant effect. This is an immense misguided judgment; it drives us to believe that we should experience hardship in order to succeed. I don't believe you should feel that you should be adhered to casualty mode to claim the force of your story. It likewise doesn't need to include a tremendous Hollywood snare. You don't need to leave your place of employment and sell all that you own, have a profound excursion around Europe, do some kind of wild climb across the Pacific Peak Trail, carry on with a legendary sentiment, or have a colossal montage set to 80's music. Each story is novel and you can have profound changes occurring with the least complex circumstances.

One way or the other you have a story to tell and the world needs to hear it at whatever point you are prepared. Since you likewise don't need to narrate a story you're not prepared to tell.

The Power behind Your Story

The most important part about your story is that it's credible. Your reality motivates and mends. Recall that you arrived today in view of the relative multitude of examples you have learned, and those illustrations hold the ability to help other people. It additionally holds the capacity to release your skill.

Nobody has the extraordinary combo of range of abilities and story that you do. There is in a real sense nobody on this whole planet that can give your very best! Isn't that astonishing? Just you can do, initiate and make something great with your abilities and vision. You know that expression "It's completely been done before"? well no doubt, all that has been finished previously, however not by you. Your story has the supernatural ability to open another entryway. It has the force of another point of view that nobody has at any point seen or known about.

At the point when you own your story, you are claiming what your identity is, and by honoring and respecting your expedition (the promising and less promising times), you open your actual potential, and in that lies allure.

Claiming Your Story

There's power in narrating. Imparting your life into the world is difficult yet it's important to both you and others. Claiming your story is significant in your very own development and it assists with making profound associations with your local area.

Here is the unnerving part, possessing your story is tolerating yourself as you are. Your crude, wonderful, fragile self. The muddled considerations, the difficulties, the extreme illustrations, every last bit of it. It takes guts, endlessly parcel of guts, weakness, and a ton of here-goes-nothing motivational speeches. At last, when you share your reality, it seems like enchantment.

In some cases claiming your story implies sharing the chaotic, not-really lovely pieces of you. In any case, it will remind others that you're human as well, that we as a whole are a work underway.

Once in a while it implies not sharing that ideal Instagram post and allowing the genuine you to sparkle and advance the made-up existent factors of the social application. In any case, it will give others the boldness to share their genuine selves as well.

Some of the time it's recommended to tell yourself that where you've been isn't where you're going and you have the ability to adjust your course at any moment. It will show others how we're the creators of our own lives and we have the ability to transform them.

At times you must be courageous and uncover it all so another person can feel less alone. Other times, you need to face yourself with fortitude and thoughtfulness so you can break through your restricting convictions and let your actual self radiate through.

Stories hold power. In this day and age we hunger for validness and association, we need to feel understood. I realize that checking a blogger's post about how she endured tension with Instagram caused me to feel less alone. It caused me to feel like I wasn't strange for feeling such about an application. It gave me the fortitude to bring it down and to cleanse it from my life. It was practically similar to the consent I expected to conflict with society and my own apprehensions and simply eliminate it from my life.

Stories arouse stories, so I welcome you to take advantage of your local area this week and offer your story. Whether it's your full biography or a solitary encounter, open up. When you share your story, you urge others to do likewise and that is supernatural.

CHAPTER 2

TRACKING DOWN SATISFACTION

Achievement customarily has been characterized by money and power. It's arriving at the top, ordering the room, purchasing that Rolex, and moving into a major house on the hill. Yet, I'm determined to get however many individuals as I can to quit looking for progress and begin searching for satisfaction.

With the high speed of regular day-to-day existence, it's not difficult to get an inclination as though you're falling behind. Finding satisfaction in life can be extremely hard when one doesn't feel stable ground under the foot.

Competitors, specifically, carry on with an exceptionally cutthroat way of life and could experience the ill effects of not feeling satisfied. Since the vast majority of their life's emphasis is on results, difficulties they experience (like a terrible instructional meeting or over-preparing) carry substantially more weight.

After not approaching expected results, a few competitors could try and feel they are not sufficient or not commendable or a 'disappointment'. Such considerations can without much of a stretch killjoy in and get horrendous on the off chance that we let them.

Finding Satisfaction in Life Is a Continuous Cycle

Negative considerations can enhance with the utilization of web-based entertainment, which keeps an eye on features indisputably the most awesome aspects of life. As we manage our everyday battles simply to fall into the mindset that others' lives are considerably more intriguing or don't have that numerous issues.

The main thing about joy, satisfaction, and sensation of achievement is that they never come from an external perspective. They must be created from the inside.

It's all about staying focused on our life. Searching for what moves us and flashes energy. About making encounters of various sorts, since that is what adds significance to life.

The following are approaches to tracking down satisfaction throughout everyday life, as well as certain thoughts that would assist with adding importance to daily happenings and help to live more in the moment.

Challenge Yourself to Develop

Bliss is a result of an activity. Make steps towards satisfaction by taking part in the endless course of personal development.

Stay open to groundbreaking insights and thoughts, remain hungry for information, and try to do what you say others should do. You can continuously improve to an expert and a superior individual.

Improve Other People

Legitimate satisfaction comes from adding to other people. Individuals appreciate participating in charity work since it both helps other people feel better and feels noble.

Charitable activities cause us to feel more associated and build our sympathy for individuals' special encounters. Confronting the existential truth of our own finitude helps our capacity to make significant associations with others, which opens our hearts and adjusts our point of view on life.

Live Right Now

Relinquish your endless self-talk. Enjoy some time off without looking at the unending diversion of your iPhone. Stop, and simply be available.

At the point when an old computer has such a large number of projects running simultaneously, it slows down. The more that you can interface with the tranquility of the present time and place, the lower your nervousness and disappointment, and the more prominent your focus.

At the point when you're submerged in the present moment, your efficiency and bliss will soar.

End Your Propensity for Self-Absorption

A large portion of us feels like we "ought to have" certain things occur. We "ought to have" gotten that advancement; we "ought to have" felt appreciated for our great deed; we "ought to have" had additional opportunity to fulfill a time constraint.

In all actuality, we build the little space to which we're detained. At the point when we set assumptions for what ought to occur, we add to feeling baffled, restless, and discouraged.

We want to move our concentration to what is and begin being thankful for what we have as opposed to agonizing over what we don't.

Interface with an Option Bigger Than Yourself

Just as giving assists us with feeling more sympathetic with others and keen on what we have, here and there it means quite a bit to feel how little our concerns truly are.

At the point when you drench yourself in the mountains or swim in the immeasurability of the sea, you understand how negligible your protests are over the long haul. We frequently empower our concerns and make them bigger than they should be.

On the off chance that achievement and satisfaction make our lives advantageous, we want to return issues to their appropriate spot.

Have a Character

Our one-of-a-kind character is shaped by our qualities, things we're keen on, and the standards we keep.

Be that as it may, we live in a world overwhelmed by sentiments, promotion, and peer pressure. In some cases, the outer message is clearly to such an extent 'that an individual is pushed to acknowledge something he's not enthusiastic about.

Knowing what your identity is is a big motivator for you, and possessing it takes certainty. Our inward voice generally understands what's best for ourselves and doing things as we would prefer acquires significantly more satisfaction than fitting.

Try not to accomplish something every other person appears to. Find a side interest you appreciate and a community that moves you.

Track Down Your Way

One extraordinary approach to finding satisfaction in life is characterizing a dream (and getting it on paper). Its a useful asset that guides organizations through tough situations and it's considerably more powerful for individuals.

Have you at any point contemplated what you uphold that your life should be about? What truly matters to you? What does the ideal day look like for you? What gives you joy and you might want to have a greater amount of it?

These are the absolute hardest inquiries to honestly address. Be that as it may, answers assist with directing your day-to-day existence. Does what you do consistently add to your vision? In the event that is not, find measured ways to improve it.

Have a Strict Arrangement at the Top of the Priority List

Arranging rejuvenates thoughts and wants. Plunk down with a scratch pad, ponder and record what is it that you need to accomplish in seven days, months, years, 5 years, or even 10 years.

Having even an obscure thought about where you're going assists with remaining on track. Likewise, essentially expressing your desires to yourself makes a magical difference. Some way or another, the universe generally gives amazing chances to get things going.

Put Forth More Modest and More Feasible Objectives

A drawn-out plan of where you need to go is something worth being thankful for. In any case, in general, it's simply this one feared thing you need to accomplish, yet are not even close to. It could be extremely scary to the point that you don't have confidence in it yourself.

Splitting the arrangement into numerous more modest and effectively feasible objectives creates stepping stones to that gigantic unapproachable cliff. It serves to completely zero in on the ongoing work and later value all the difficult work.

At the point when I concocted the plan to complete an Ironman, it felt exceptionally scary (12+ long hours of activity are serious stuff). In any case, after finishing 3 long-distance races, crashing in my first marathon, and completing a half Ironman race, the entire thought didn't appear to be that insane any longer.

Celebrate

With a high speed of life, we're constantly centered around the future and where we need to get. In any case, as the time elapses, as a rule, we notice that the expedition was as a matter of fact the objective.

As a serious competitor, I used to be caught in this perspective for a really long time. I generally felt I wasn't sufficient and am simply permitted to celebrate once I win or accomplish the most elevated desire I set for myself.

The issue with this perspective is that until you accomplish your major objective you're distressed. In this way, as a general rule, I had a severe trailing sensation after what, as a matter of fact, was a very decent performance.

Defining more modest objectives gives many motivations to celebrate and appreciate where you came from. Reward yourself for more modest accomplishments and don't generally be 'trapped' from here on out.

Never Equate and Live Where You Are

Contrasting yourself is equivalent to living in the future while caught in the present. Or on the other hand more regrettable - previously. At the point when we contrast ourselves with something we accept is better, we get sincerely connected to that condition and get detached from our existence. The greater the distinction, the higher the disappointment.

Finding satisfaction in human existence has a meaning that transcends quantifying against others or what we used to be or even where we'd need to be. It's tied in with playing the card we manage and residing where we're right now. Not where we figure we could be or where online entertainment lets us think we ought to be.

Accepting that is the hardest part, as the media generally attempts to let us know how we ought to manage our time and cash or even what we ought to think. In the event that outer pressure is too high, a digital detox may be an extraordinary method for hitting relief and focus on what gives you joy instead.

Appreciate, Don't Say Anything Negative

Grumbling is simple, which is the reason it's a standard reaction to a sensation of disappointment, discontent, being furious, and so on. It's just a simple approach to offering pessimistic viewpoints and feelings. Griping is a disastrous propensity and whining all the more just develops a negative manner of thinking.

Then again, being appreciative of what occurs in our lives and what we have is extremely strong at providing us with the control of our joy. Contemplate everything that made you what your identity is. Without a doubt there have been both great and terrible encounters en route - appreciate that. The more we figure out how to let go in the moment, the more joyful we will be.

Look For Bliss First, All the Other Things Second

Accomplishing something that flashes enthusiasm or euphoria is an incredible method for creating energy and positive inspiration. That likewise assists with remaining predictable with the propensity or practice in any event, when things get somewhat unpleasant.

Ensure you have a good time consistently both with others and with yourself. Our view of reality turns into our world. Thus, when we center around satisfying every other person but us, we gamble to lose that feeling of play that gives existence its tones.

Doing what you disregard is a catastrophe waiting to happen. Assuming that you'll burn through 10+ hours consistently cycling, running, and kayaking you ought to enjoy the actual process. Not just outcomes that it brings.

Investigate Different Leisure Activities

Make every moment count. The key to lasting satisfaction is straightforward. Find whatever motivates you and try to do that consistently. Both for work and as a side interest.

On the off chance that is conceivable, attempt to shake things up, so that you're not generally centered around exactly the same thing. Enjoying assorted leisure activities assists with getting some viewpoint on what truly interests and ignites enthusiasm for us.

Proficient competitors, for example, ought to find something other than training as a side interest (cooking, perhaps?). Individuals with exceptionally 'quantitative' work (for example bookkeepers, investigators, and so on), on the other hand, might look into discovering their creative side (like composition or drawing).

Have an Insane or Unnerving Escapade as a Primary Concern (Or Both)

Life ought not to be all serious constantly. Having fantasy or an insane experience on a list of must-dos adds a touch of a rush to your life and could try and assist with finding new interests.

This experience ought to be something that panics you somewhat but above all something that you feel intrigued by. It very well may be all around as intense as paddling across the Atlantic Sea or in any event, cycling from Europe to Asia.

Frequently pondering and arranging such awe-inspiring experiences causes individuals to understand that large dreams are a lot nearer than they show up.

Make Equilibrium throughout Everyday Life

The test (or rather a magnificence) of life is that there's actually no need to focus on accomplishing one scorch objective. Otherwise, all rich people and celebrities would be cheerful.

In actuality, satisfaction traverses across different everyday issues and is consistently a mix of different variables. We can't zero in just on a solitary region, in light of the fact that eventually, we'll feel unfulfilled in others. For example, being rich wouldn't mean a thing in the event that one doesn't have a family or a gathering of companions who care about him to impart it to. Very much like working a ton to have a fruitful profession to the detriment of individual wellbeing.

Each individual has their own recipe; however, finding satisfaction in life comes down to investing energy into everything about the regions beneath:

- Family (associations with close family)
- Work and profession (accomplishments, individual activities, and so forth.)
- Physical (wellbeing and prosperity)
- Scholarly (learning and self-improvement)
- Social (associations with others, societal position)
- Profound (self-revelation, mindfulness)

- Monetary

Help Other People Magnanimously

Disregard the possibility that somebody owes you something throughout everyday life. Regardless of whether extensively, it's valid.

Be liberal all things considered. Help other people without anticipating anything subsequently. Give gifts to other people. Dedicate time and consideration regarding the ones you love and the individuals with who you don't actually have the foggiest idea. That is the key to making genuine significance and tracking down satisfaction throughout everyday life.

Surprisingly, the delight of making another person blissful creates satisfaction for yourself.

Finding satisfaction in life is dependably about more than just yourself. There's little more satisfaction than realizing you've had an effect on somebody's life.

Set Aside Time for Yourself

Try not to hold on to finish all that's on your plan for the day or satisfy everyone before taking care of yourself. All things being equal, put time oftentimes into self-improvement. Be it reading, exercising, or individual activities. Whenever you're fulfilled, you'll have more energy to help other people.

Personally, I like to invest energy in my own activities promptly in the first part of the day. That way I can concentrate on expanded timeframes, as there are fewer interruptions and nothing else to do.

Have a Strong Community

However much we let ourselves know we can make it all alone, individuals are social generally and we want to connect with others.

Notwithstanding, it's essential to invest energy with the right sort of individuals - the people who support your interests and leisure activities, rather than chuckling at them. Individuals that will assist you with developing as an expert and personally.

They say you're the average of 5 individuals you invest the most time with. In the advanced age, however, it's not just them any longer. It's also who you decide to follow, cooperate and connect yourself with.

In this way, encircle yourself with the sort of individuals you respect and turn upward to. Join conversation/interest/plan bunches that you are keen on and limit the time you enjoy with individuals who adversely impact you.

Tidy Up Your Eating Routine

Our eating routine generally characterizes how great we feel and how amazing we are. Furthermore, that directly affects our fruitfulness.

Weighty (protein-rich) and exceptionally handled feasts put a ton of weight on the body by establishing an acidic climate and causing irritation. Handling food likewise requires a ton of energy and, whenever eaten excessively near sleep time, weakens rest quality. All of this adversely influences our safe framework, yet also our mindset.

The speediest method for being better, feeling improved, and having more energy is to add more plant-based feasts into your eating routine. In addition to the fact that it is really great for yourself, it is, also for the environment

Work Out

Moving the body animates the blood flow to muscles and organs, which makes them work all the more proficiently. The impact is as though you're having an extra chance of energy.

While you're feeling short on energy or genuinely down (encountering a 'killjoy'), one of the most outstanding fixes is to move the body. For example, take an energetic walk/run or do a yoga meeting.

Additionally, higher force practice animates chemical creation that keeps us more youthful and feeling more joyful. Not to mention the good discussions and laughs you'll get by training in a group.

.

Invest Energy in Nature

Nature has an extraordinary ability to quiet down and re-energize both the body and the spirit. Aside from getting outside air and, most presumably, working out, investing energy in nature assists with logging off from whatever is going on throughout everyday life.

It doesn't need to be a fantastic spot high in the mountains or a secret ocean side someplace in Bali to give mending power. A basic stroll in the park or the backwoods is all that could possibly be needed. It's valuing nature and investing energy without gadgets that do the magic.

Focus On Rest

A large percentage of persons don't get sufficient rest. What's more, numerous who really do need more supportive rest? You know, the one after which you feel in your prime and ready for business.

Helpful rest yields more resolve, permits more readily answers ordinary burdens and further develops wellbeing, mindset, and efficiency. Several fixes can essentially work on the nature of rest, which has a monstrous impact on general prosperity and personal satisfaction. Why not make that a day-to-day practice?

Have a Learning Attitude

As a last, however, I need to leave you with this.

Challenge yourself to develop. Focus on it to get out of your usual range of familiarity and discover some new information. Feel free to commit errors. It's not possible for anyone to try not to make those throughout everyday life, other than the people who never have a go at a novel, new thing.

Enduring is important for the human condition. Searching for joy beyond yourself adds to hopelessness and leads to lamentation towards the expiration of life.

Quit expecting and begin appreciating. Quit contemplating what "ought to be" and begin being appreciative of "what is." The more you can keep learning and developing, the more joyful you'll turn into.

At the point when you challenge yourself to develop, add to other people, and live right now, you will work on your efficiency and develop a feeling of satisfaction.

Subsequent to finishing your propensity for self-absorption and altering your point of view on your concerns, you'll be prepared to obtain riches and the one thing cash can't purchase - satisfaction.

CHAPTER 3

LAY OUT YOUR LIFE MISSION

On the off chance that you don't feel satisfied by or content with your life, you might choose to assess your life's resolution. While this can be a difficult self-assessment that might persuade you to think that you've been carrying on with life the "incorrect way," cheer up; it's never past the time to start carrying on with your desired life to live a day to day existence that is significant and blissful. Find your life's motivation, then make a move to carry out the sort of everyday routine you truly need to experience.

For anybody who is looking to work on themselves, accomplish better outcomes in life or partake in meaningful personal progress, there is one essential question to ask yourself: **what is my life goal?** The response is, as a matter of fact, of mind-boggling significance, as it turns into the establishment for any remaining exercises you will embrace in your life. The response will turn into your compass. It will direct your exercises, give importance to your life and fix fatigue and disappointment.

Fruitful business pioneers know that to accomplish extraordinary outcomes in that business, they would be advised to grasp the reason for that business. On the off chance that you're hoping to acknowledge unbelievable outcomes from your life, shouldn't you have a reason, as well?

Where does my life reason come from?

Nobody is holding on to give you your life motivation. You pick it. This is immensely enabling and a magnificent disclosure. Your life purpose will act as the reason for how you carry on with your existence. Your objectives and activities will be in every way lined up with your life purpose. Your ways of behaving, values, decisions, and bliss will all equally work together with your life reason. So pick smartly.

In spite of the staggering effect of having a huge life purpose, there is definitely not a definite fire technique for nurturing the most ideal life reason proclamation for everybody.

Also, life purposes can and ought to change over the long haul. Subsequently, this is a singular activity, permitting you to be innovative and pick one that works for you. The technique that works for you currently may not be best for your companions. It might likewise not be best for a future variant of you. Hence, I offer here 5 methods for making your life reason.

1. Make a rundown of activities that satisfy you

"Genuine satisfaction isn't accomplished through self-delight, yet through devotion to a worthy purpose."

The more you carry on with your life making progress toward bigger importance and reason, the more joyful you will be. In like manner, what satisfies you is subsequently a sign of what your specific reason in life is. Work out a rundown of what makes you genuinely cheerful and joyful. By participating in this activity and routinely auditing the rundown, your life reason might leap out at you.

Achievement follows satisfaction.

"On account of this state-of-the-art science, we currently realize that satisfaction is the precursor to progress, not simply the outcome."

2. Make a list of what has caused you to feel eager to get up

"The secret of human life lies not in remaining alive, but rather finding something to live for."

Here is one more rundown to make. Reminisce through your life, back to when you were a kid. Find those times in your day-to-day existence when you kept awake until late energetically associated with something, just to awaken excited and eager to begin once more. Record as lengthy of a rundown as could really be expected and survey it routinely. Likewise with number 1, hope to track down shared characteristics and draw nearer to your life's motivation.

3. Inquire why you're exceptional

In the event that your life design is picked by you, explicitly for you, and can and ought to be unique in relation to every other person's, you would be advised to take advantage of your natural abilities. What are you generally excellent at comparing with others? Just sit back and relax in the event that they're senseless things or less important according to other people. This is you.

4. Characterize your ideal presence

Accepting no impediments, what might your ideal life resemble? Work out your fantasy story. In the case everything was great, what might your life resemble in 10 years? Who is a major part of your life? Where are you residing? How would you add to society?

5. Plug into the remainder of the world

Genuine joy doesn't come from being narcissistic. Your life reason requires you to incorporate a significant commitment to everyone around you. Who would you like to help? How would you like to help them? Educating? Assistance? Charity of cash? How can your unique resources help others?

Begin Tracking down Your Purpose and Open Your Best Life

Finding purpose in life is something that the vast majority need. Regardless of whether we know it. As decent as it sounds, it can appear to be challenging to achieve.

On the off chance that you haven't invested a great deal of energy contemplating your own drive, you could have a few assumptions about the reason for life. These prepared thoughts regarding life frequently come from our family and the networks we experience childhood in. The reason for our life is to get hitched and have children. Or on the other hand, perhaps it's making a specific measure of money or accomplishing a specific position in the public eye.

However, these sorts of accomplishments frequently don't bring the sort of satisfaction that accompanies discovering your own feeling of direction.

An individual feeling of direction is to a lesser degree a particular ultimate objective and a greater amount of a continuous effect on the world, huge or little. Your drive is your why.

This individual feeling of direction directs and supports you. Every day and as the years advances. In any event, when you have mishaps and the world flips around, your purpose gives you strength and an internal compass. That is the reason finding your drive is fundamental for living a blissful, sound life.

While asking what your motivation is can appear to be an elevated inquiry, it's one worth inquiring about. Also, attempting to answer. Finding your motivation can open more prominent fulfillment and progress in all parts of your life.

So let's jump into the central issues: what is purpose throughout everyday life, why it is important, and 12 moves toward tracking down your purpose.

What is the purpose behind life?

Scholars have looked for and discussed "the purpose behind life" for quite a long time. We won't attempt to respond to that here. What makes a difference is your motivation throughout everyday life.

The vast majority will ask eventually, "What am I doing here?" It very well may be a terrifying inquiry or an outright exhilarating one. Inclining toward the distress of this existential inquiry can prompt a superior identity and more rewarding ways ahead.

Your motivation in life is as extraordinary to you as your unique mark. We as a whole have a specific arrangement of gifts, encounters, ranges of abilities, and interests that light us up. Your drive is connected with these, however, it is your reason behind existence. It is the reason you get up in the first part of the day, in any event when the day is terrible, you're worn out, and you know the tasks and problems ahead will be hard or in any event, exhausting.

The intention is the big-picture approach, not the momentary objective. You never get to its furthest limit. Be that as it may, even areas of strength and of direction can wear you out. That is the reason, preferably, your motivation mixes with what intrigues you and gives you pleasure.

In Japan, this idea is known as ikigai, and it's the idea of following your bliss. Ikigai has developed well known in the West as of late as manners to assist with peopling find their fantasy vocations and professional ways.

The idea is finding the cross-over between what you love and the world's necessities with what you are great at and what the world will pay for. You create your feeling of direction from your energy as well as pragmatic contemplations.

Assuming you're fortunate, you could have found your ikigai through your work. For instance, a specialist ideally accepts their motivation is to assist with sick individuals or to ease suffering.

For other people, finding significance in our work and associating it with our own feeling of direction isn't all that simple. Between work, family obligations, and social assumptions, we frequently leave the optimistic variant of ourselves that longs to discover a feeling of importance and reason throughout everyday life. We accept we need to make this tradeoff. That importance and reason can't exist with down-to-earth contemplations. Yet, that isn't beneficial.

You want a feeling of direction to support you over the long run. Furthermore, in any event, when life feels like a progression of compromises, you can in any case find and interface with your motivation by investigating what gives you pleasure and committing additional opportunities to it.

Why is finding reason significant?

Finding your motivation in life could seem like a pleasure to have, however, it's surprisingly significant.

Carrying on with a significant life adds to better actual well-being and mental fitness. It likewise lessens the gamble of persistent sickness. Numerous investigations have even found that it can assist you with living longer.

Having a feeling of direction comes from feeling associated with others. Involving your gifts in the assistance of others can assist you with tracking down your actual reason, while separation and dejection can make you have an existential emergency.

You will likely find that your motivation changes all through your life. Consistent development and progress can assist you with remaining associated with your motivation.

The Most Effective Method to Track down Reason throughout Everyday Life

Assuming you're asking yourself, "What is my motivation?" you're in good company. One review showed that only ¼ of American grown-ups say they have a clear feeling of direction.

Assuming you're part of the other 75%, follow these tips to begin tracking down reason and significance throughout everyday life.

1. Nurture a development outlook

Having a development outlook is connected to having a feeling of direction. Continually developing and improving as a rendition of yourself assists you with recognizing your motivation and focusing on chasing after it.

A development mentality likewise permits you to:

- Embrace difficulties as an open door
- Persist in disregarding disappointment
- Acknowledge input and productive analysis

2. Make an individual vision proclamation

An individual vision clarification can assist you with overseeing pressure and tracking down balance in your life. It likewise fills in as a guide that will direct you toward your motivation by recognizing your basic beliefs and laying out what means quite a bit to you.

A goal explanation makes it more straightforward for you to go with choices adjusted to your qualities and assists you with remaining inspired as you pursue your own objectives.

3. Give back

Giving back, or prosocial behavior as it's known in psychology, can improve your feeling of importance and reason throughout everyday life. This implies that when you help other people, you additionally help yourself.

Search for ways to help out. You should chip in your nearby local area or give your cash or abilities to a reason that impacts you. Or on the other hand, have a go at spreading a little joy by performing random thoughtful gestures.

4. Practice appreciation

The prosociality investigation discovered that zeroing in on appreciation not withstanding demonstrations of charitableness reinforced the members' feeling of direction.

Another review uncovered that appreciation actuates similar prize reactions in the cerebrum as prosocial conduct.

It likewise found that developing appreciation can make you more liberal and lead to thoughtful gestures, which we currently know adds to discovering a feeling of direction.

Rehearsing appreciation can feel a piece off-kilter from the outset. We get so used to our negative contemplations that exchanging them for good ones can feel unnatural.

To begin, take a shot at composing three to five things you feel thankful for a first thing in the morning or around evening time before you nod off.

5. Transform your aggravation into motivation

We as a whole face battles throughout everyday life. Conquering these difficulties shapes who we become and gives us our novel assets and viewpoints. Many individuals request help while attempting to defeat a significant life-altering event. Some later find their motivation in helping other people confronting comparative battles to those they have survived. Some pick a profession working directly with individuals, for example, a holistic mentor or social laborer. Others track down ways of contacting the existences of others through artistic expressions, like composition, painting, or music. A few become inspirational orators.

How you change your aggravation into a drive depends on you.

6. Explore your interests

Your interests and wellbeing are a decent sign of the area wherein your life's reason could lie. However, they can be difficult to recognize. They're so imbued in our ways of reasoning that we can become unmindful to them. On the off chance that you don't know what your interests are, ask individuals who realize you best. Probably, you're now chasing after them here and there without acknowledging it. Maybe you're an informal coach to youngsters locally. Assuming this is the case, that could be your obsession.

One more method for finding your enthusiasm is to contemplate what you're great at. Somebody who's perfect at helping other people tackle their concerns should think about a profession as a mentor. You could like to keep your passion as a leisure activity, or you could choose to transform it into a side gig or full-time source of income.

7. Be connected to a community

Purpose is tied in with feeling associated with others, so being a functioning individual from a community can add to a more prominent feeling of direction throughout everyday life.

At the point when you find your motivation, you'll find that there are numerous others out there who share your interests, desires, and values. Joining or making a community permits you to discover that feeling of association with others as you cooperate toward a shared objective.

8. Invest energy with individuals who motivate you

You are the average of the five individuals you invest the most energy with. On the off chance that you invest energy with individuals who are positive and reason driven, they are probably going to motivate you to have a similar mentality. You might try and find your motivation through them.

Look past your partners and relatives and ask yourself who you decide to invest your energy with. Assess those connections and ensure you are encircling yourself with optimistic, positive individuals who lift you up.

9. Peruse

One of the most amazing ways of extending your psychological skylines is through understanding fiction. Genuine books are helpful for getting information on specific subjects. However, research recommends that perusing fiction might have more advantages.

Perusing fiction works on your sympathy and basic and imaginative reasoning. This is on the grounds that when you put yourself in the shoes of a person, you envision how you would respond to that.

Perusing likewise associates you with others across time, place, and societies. This assists you with developing the feeling of connectedness that produces a feeling of direction throughout everyday life.

10. Join a cause

We as a whole have a cause that we feel energetically about. Maybe you have particular inclinations toward civil rights, animal welfare, or the climate.

Battling for a purpose integrates a few of the tips referenced above, including:

- Giving back
- Forming a community
- Doing something you're zealous about
- Encircling yourself with individuals who motivate you

Perhaps you need to fund-raise for an investigation into a specific illness or give ghetto kids access to green spaces. Anything it is, engaging with a purpose will assist you with tracking down more reasons in your life.

11. Practice self-acknowledgment

Accepting your restrictions can assist you with being kinder to yourself when things turn out badly. We as a whole commit errors, however rather than pounding yourself for your disappointments, attempt to consider every misfortune to be a valuable chance to develop.

Self-empathy can assist you with turning out to be more mindful and self-tolerating. At the point when you acknowledge yourself, you're all bound to give the best of yourself in each circumstance. This may be at work, with your family, or while doing the things you love. This can prompt a more noteworthy feeling of association with others and all that you do, giving more importance to your life.

12. Set aside some time for taking care of oneself

Taking care of oneself comes in many structures, and your variant of taking care of oneself is extraordinary to you. Maybe you like strolling in the backwoods, rehearsing some profound breathing, or journaling out your troublesome feelings.

Be that as it may, for what reason is taking care of oneself significant? Since when our minds are loose, they are at their generally inventive. You can't accomplish or serve others when you are fighting against yourself.

Have you at any point seen that a portion of your smartest thoughts come when you're in the shower? That is on the grounds that our brains are more open and responsive to the progression of thoughts than they are at the point at which we attempt to drive ourselves to think. Imaginative reasoning works out easily when our psyches are in a condition of unwinding. Furthermore, it can lead you nearer to tracking down your motivation.

Finding Determination in Life Doesn't Have To Be Hard

Behind each fruitful individual is a clearness of direction. Also, except if you see it as yours, you'll keep on cruising through life on autopilot. You might wind up knocked off kilter and lost, uncertain on how to push ahead or which course to follow. Or on the other hand, life might be smooth however one day you might think back and wish you had utilized your time in an unexpected way.

Recognizing, pinpointing, and regarding your motivation is the foundation of a balanced life. It requires some boldness since it opens up questions and thoughts that probably won't be agreeable. However, it's worth the effort. Purpose furnishes you with an internal compass that directs each choice and leads you to the encounters that will illuminate your spirit.

CHAPTER 4

BALANCE BETWEEN WORK AND LIFE ACTIVITIES

Balance between fun and serious activities alludes to the degree of prioritization among individual and expert exercises in one's life and the level to which exercises connected with their occupation are available in the home.

The ideal balance between fun and serious activities is available for conversation. Anthropologists frequently characterize satisfaction as having practically zero separation between ones expert and individual lives.

Balance between serious and fun activities is an effective issue because of the expanded measure of innovation that eliminates the significance of the actual area in characterizing the balance between serious and fun activities. Beforehand it was troublesome or difficult to bring work back home thus there was an evident line between experts and individual lives.

The expansion in portable innovation, cloud-based programming, and the multiplication of the web has made it a lot simpler for representatives to be 'for all time' at work, obscuring the differentiation among experts and individual lives. A few observers contend that cell phones and 'always on' access to the working environment have displaced the authoritarian control of bosses.

Stress is a typical component of an unfortunate balance between fun and serious activities. In the data economy, mental pressure has been distinguished as a huge monetary and medical condition, made by an apparent need for representatives to accomplish more quickly than expected.

A central question in the balance between fun and serious activities banter is where the obligation lies for guaranteeing representatives have a decent balance between serious and fun activities. The general inclination is that businesses have an obligation to the soundness of their representatives; aside from the ethical obligation, worried workers are not so useful but rather more liable to make blunders.

Adjusting your expert and individual life can be testing, yet all the same, it's fundamental. This is the way to further develop your balance between fun and serious activities today.

Frequently, work outweighs all the other things in our lives. Our longing to succeed expertly can push us to save our own prosperity. Making an amicable balance between fun and serious activities or work-life combination is basic; however, to work on not just our physical, profound, and mental prosperity, but on the other hand, it's significant for our vocation.

What is balance between fun and serious activities and for what reason is it significant?

To put it plainly, balance between fun and serious activities is the condition of harmony where an individual similarly focuses on the requests of one's vocation and the requests of one's very own life. A portion of the normal reasons that lead to an unfortunate balance between serious and fun activities include:

- Expanded liabilities at work
- Working longer hours
- Expanded liabilities at home
- Having kids

A decent balance between fun and serious activities makes various positive impacts, including less pressure, a lower chance of burnout, and a more prominent feeling of prosperity. This advantages workers as well as bosses.

Businesses who are focused on giving conditions that help balance between serious and fun activities for their representatives can save money on costs, experience fewer instances of non-appearance, and partake in a more steadfast and useful labor force.

While making a timetable that works for you, contemplate the most ideal way to accomplish balance at work and in your own life. Balance between fun and serious activities is less about partitioning the hours in your day equally among work and individual life and, all things considered, is more about having the adaptability to finish things in your expert life while as yet having the investment to partake in your own life.

There might be a few days where you work long hours so you have time later in the week to appreciate different exercises.

Here are ways of making a superior balance between serious and fun activities, as well as how to be a strong supervisor.

1. Acknowledge that there is no perfect balance between serious and fun activities.

At the point when you hear "balance between serious and fun activities," you presumably envision having a very useful day at work and leaving ahead of schedule to enjoy the other portion of the day with loved ones. While this might appear to be great, it is absurd 100% of the time.

Try not to take a stab at the ideal timetable; make progress toward a reasonable one. Every so often, you could zero in more on work, while on different days you could have additional significant investment to seek after your leisure activities or invest energy with your friends and family. Balance is accomplished over the long run, not every day.

It is critical to stay liquid and continually survey where you are your objectives and needs. On occasion, your kids might require you, and at different times, you might have to go to work, however permitting yourself to stay open to diverting and surveying your necessities on any day is key in tracking down balance.

2. Get a line of work that you love.

In spite of the fact that work is a normal cultural standard, your profession ought not to be limiting. Assuming you disdain what you do, you won't be blissful, plain and simple. You don't have to cherish each part of your work, yet it should be energizing enough that you don't fear getting up each day.

Getting a new line of work that you are so energetic about is suggested because you would do it for nothing. On the off chance that your occupation is depleting you, and you are finding it hard to do the things you love beyond work, something is off-base.

You might be working in a toxic environment, for a toxic individual, or finishing a work that you really don't cherish. If so, the time has come to get another line of work.

3. Focus on your well-being.

Your general physical, mental, and emotional well-being ought to be your fundamental concern. Assuming you battle with uneasiness or sorrow schedule, fit those meetings into your timetable, regardless of whether you need to go home early or ditch your night-turn class. In the event that you are fighting a constant disease, make it a point to phone in on unpleasant days. Exhausting yourself keeps you from improving, possibly making you take more days off in the future.

Focusing on your wellbeing will make you a superior representative and individual. Most importantly, you will miss less work, and when you are there, you will be more joyful and useful.

Focusing on your well-being doesn't need to comprise revolutionary or outrageous exercises. It can be as straightforward as everyday reflection or exercise.

4. Make it a point to turn off.

Cutting binds with the rest of the world occasionally permits us to recuperate from the week-by-week stress and gives us space for different contemplations and thoughts to arise. Turning off can mean something straightforward like rehearsing travel reflection on your everyday drive, rather than browsing work messages.

Mess around, read a book. Figure out how to de-pressurize and offer yourself a reprieve rather than continuously being lowered in something business related in this manner driving yourself to potential burnout. Finding an opportunity to loosen up is basic to progress and will assist you with feeling more empowered when you're at work.

5. Getaway.

Now and then, genuinely turning off implies taking downtime and closing work totally off for some time. Whether your getaway comprises a one-day vacation or a two-week excursion to Bali, it's vital to take time off to genuinely and intellectually re-energize.

Employees are in many cases stressed that getting some much-needed rest will disturb the work process, and they will be met with a build-up of work when they return. This dread shouldn't confine you from having some long overdue time off.

Truly, there is no honorability in not removing merited time from work; the advantages of going home for the day far offset the disadvantages. With legitimate preparation, you can remove time without stressing over, troubling your partners or fighting with an immense responsibility when you return.

6. Set aside some time for you as well as your friends and family.

While your occupation is significant, it ought not to be as long as you can remember. You were a person prior to taking this position, and you ought to focus on the exercises or leisure activities that satisfy you. Accomplishing a balance between serious and fun activities requires conscious activity.

In the event that you don't solidly make arrangements for individual time, you won't have the opportunity to do different things beyond work. Regardless of how feverish your timetable may be, you, at last, have control of your time and life.

While arranging a time with your friends and family, make a schedule for heartfelt and family dates. It might appear to be strange to design one-on-one time with somebody you live with, yet it will guarantee that you invest quality energy with them without work-life struggle. Since work keeps you occupied, that doesn't mean you ought to disregard individual connections.

Understand that nobody at your organization will cherish you or value you the manner in which your friends and family do. Likewise remember that everybody is replaceable at work, and regardless of how significant you think your occupation is the organization won't overlook anything tomorrow assuming you are no more.

7. **Put down stopping points and work hours.**

Put down stopping points for you as well as your partners, to stay balanced. At the point when you leave the workplace, abstain from pondering impending undertakings or noting work messages. Consider having a different computer or telephone for work, so you can shut it down when you call it a day. In the event that that isn't possible, utilize separate programs, messaging applications, or channels for your work and personal platforms.

Furthermore, setting explicit work hours is suggested. Whether you work away from home or at home, it is vital to decide when you will work and when you will quit working; if not, you could end up going through business-related messages late around evening time, during excursions, or on the ends of the week off.

It's fitting to advise colleagues and your supervisor about limits past which you can't be available in light of the fact that you are participating in private exercises. This will assist with guaranteeing that they comprehend and regard your working environment, cutoff points and assumptions.

8. Put forth objectives and boundaries and stick to them.

Put forth attainable objectives by carrying out time-usage procedures, examining your plan for the day, and removing errands that have next to zero worth.

Focus on when you are generally useful working and block that downtime for your most significant business-related exercises. Try not to browse your messages and telephone at regular intervals, as those are significant time-squandering errands that crash your consideration and efficiency. Organizing your day can increment efficiency at work, which can bring about more extra energy to loosen up beyond work.

The Ascent of the Adaptable Working Environment

The individuals who really do keep an effective harmony between themselves frequently highlight their adaptable plans for getting work done. Ongoing exploration found that in the past seven years, numerous businesses has permitted laborers more noteworthy adaptability both with their schedule and where they work.

Obviously bosses keep on battling with fewer assets for benefits that cause an immediate expense. In any case, they have focused on it to give workers admittance to a more extensive assortment of advantages that fit their individual and family needs and that work on their wellbeing and prosperity.

Adaptability can pay off for bosses over the long haul. As we look forward, obviously to stay serious, businesses should track down ways of offering adaptable work choices if they have any desire to draw in and hold top skill. Balance between fun and serious activities will mean various things to various individuals in light of the fact that all things considered, we as a whole have different life responsibilities. In our consistent world, balance is an extremely private thing, and no one but you can conclude the way of life that suits you best.

Step-By-Step Instructions to Be a Supportive Boss

1. Know what your representatives are taking a stab at. Not every person has a similar balance between serious and fun activities objectives. Converse with every representative about their goals, and afterward, figure out how you might help them. A few representatives might profit from working several days every week, while others might favor modifying their day-to-day work plan. It's vital to be liberal and adaptable.

2. Set a genuine model. Your representatives take cues from you. Assuming you send messages at all hours of day and night or work all through weekends, your staffs might feel that is what is generally expected of them, as well.

3. Let workers understand what their choices are. While managers normally work effectively of featuring their balance between serious and fun activities and

4. contributions to imminent work applicants, the equivalent can't be said for imparting those drives to current employees. Consistently talk about with your workers the choices that are accessible to them. Additionally, plunk down with prospective guardians and talk about parental leave choices.
5. Stay at the forefront. It means to keep ahead on the ball on arising balance between fun and serious activity patterns. What turns out today for employees probably won't be a good fit a year later. Keeping your balance between fun and serious activities drives new, and offers popular advantages. Also, consider offering work-life programs.

CHAPTER 5

CREATE ENERGY TO ACHIEVE YOUR GOALS

Procedures to Gather Momentum throughout Everyday Life and Make Progress

Energy is basically the power made by a moving item. You probably found out about this idea in your secondary school physical science class, however, the force goes a long way past the laws of motion. Forces, when applied to thoughts of inspiration, empower you to begin thinking plainly, see that your objectives are reachable, and discover a feeling of direction, power, and course. Figuring out how to gather momentum is, hence, quite possibly the earliest move toward making progress throughout everyday life.

By gathering momentum, you are making a world in which you are more useful, more powerful, and more effective. Force assists you with moving past the underlying obstacle of not having the option to begin something and afterward pushes you all the way through. Force helps fabricate positive reasoning and energy to assist you with advancing towards your objectives.

Throughout the long term through chipping away at various undertakings and managing many individuals, I have discovered that there are three critical techniques for figuring out how to get energy and push forward.

1. Get it done

Nike's trademark is an extraordinary motto to make energy. As a matter of fact, this is one of the most mind-blowing techniques to gather momentum throughout everyday life. Whatever you need to do, whether beginning an undertaking that you have been putting off, going to the gym to shed 10 pounds, or composing the main passage of your next novel, the most effective way to gather momentum is to make a move through one little step.

By making a move, you begin to zero in your significant investment on the things that make the biggest difference.

It might feel uncomfortable right away, however, the additional significant investment you put into getting it done, the more agreeable you will begin to become with it.

After some time, the energy fabricates and takes care of itself. The more little advances you take, the more energy you will construct, the more agreeable you will do that movement or assignment, and the more useful and successful you will be.

For instance, on the off chance that you realize you have a significant work project due the following week; a little step could be to make a plan for the day of the multitude of things you'll have to do to finish the project. This will set up your brain to hop into the means the next day.

Eventually, every little step draws you nearer to accomplishing your objective, so get out there, make it happen, and join the positions of fruitful individuals giving their all to accomplish their objectives.

2. Plan It

Maybe you can't do it at this moment, yet what you can do is plan an opportunity to do that thing that you have been putting off. Shockingly better, make it a daily schedule to make energy throughout everyday life.

Assuming you have been putting off going to the gym, plan it now, and stick to it. On the off chance that you experience difficulty adhering to your timetable and not having the discipline to make a move, consider your drawn-out objectives.

Why precisely would you like to go to the exercise center, and how might your life look and feel if you shed the 10 pounds that you need to lose? On the off chance that this isn't sufficient, go ahead and reward yourself after each move that you initiate.

To truly gather momentum, you really want to make a move each and every day. One of the most outstanding ways of gathering momentum is to plan 30 minutes each day where you will be committed to what it is that you need to accomplish. All of a sudden, after a week you would have been useful for 3.5

hours! Everything adds up and making it a standard will assist with implanting it as a propensity and assist it with turning out to be important for your life.

3. Find out About It

At the point when you're not exactly ready to make a move, you can begin gathering speed by finding out what it is that you ought to do.

For instance, assuming you are attempting to get to the gym, get a well-being and wellness magazine and set out to find out about the various activities that you can embrace at the exercise center. Find out about the various projects that you can finish or the various classes that you can participate in.

Maybe you're attempting to compose the primary passage of your next novel. Get some downtime to find out about your desired theme to expound on. Get the telephone and converse with somebody about it, or peruse a site that depicts how to compose a book. Anything that it is, you can learn something about the task which will assist you with gathering momentum.

Finding out about your desired activity makes brain connections in your cerebrum that assists you with building the certainty and information to have the option to do what it is that you need to do.

To accomplish more throughout everyday life and be more successful, useful, viable, and productive, then you want to consider the above techniques to gather momentum. Recollect that once you start down away with a solitary step, you have proactively begun to gather the speed that you'll have to push you forward and finish your objectives.

CHAPTER 6

PICK APART YOUR LIFE

Do you feel like regardless of how enthusiastically you try, you're simply turning around and around, not actually getting anyplace?

You have our objectives delineated for the year, your organizers loaded up with a pink and yellow highlighter, and you know the specific guide to getting where you need to go, so for what reason is it so difficult to come by results?

Many individuals get hung up setting a lot of little, unclear, safe objectives that pull them into numerous headings and hold them back from delivering a particular outcome. We consider busyness to be something worth being thankful for, so we fill our schedules with tasks that aren't making a definite difference for ourselves and afterward get baffled when we aren't receiving results that matter. Imagine a scenario in which rather we got in on several major objectives and made an activity plan around overcoming them.

I can't let you know how frequently I've needed to turn in my business and life just to draw one stage nearer to accomplishing my fantasies. It's difficult, however, I sincerely accept that the thoughts which energize or scare us merit going after over anything more.

At the point when I think back on all that I've accomplished throughout the long term, I got going considering my final product and worked in reverse from that point. I figured out the outcomes I have in my life and I keep on working that way, crawling nearer to my fantasy life constantly.

Make your life a magnum opus; envision no impediments on what you can be, have or do

Check the Higher Perspective Out

Perhaps you don't know precisely everything where you're going, yet you realize a change is fundamental to pushing ahead in your life. Or on the other hand, perhaps you're not setting your sights sufficiently high and you're making little, achievable objectives that keep you in a similar agreeable box you've generally depended on for security.

Whichever camp you're in, you genuinely should get an obvious image of your life dreams. Make it a point to think beyond practical boundaries and set your sights high!

Snatch a diary and require a couple of moments to work out your greatest dreams without judgment. Shut your eyes and imagine yourself carrying on with your fantasy life. What does that resemble? What does that vibe like?

Plunk down, get some espresso, find a comfortable space and let yourself go in the pages of your diary. Try not to ponder it, simply compose without judgment.

Put Forth Savvy Objectives

You've most likely heard the expression "Savvy" objectives previously, maybe on the web or in a book. You continually catch wind of how brilliant objectives are the most ideal sort of objectives to set, but I'm willing to wager that you've never really made your objectives Savvy.

Time after time we get out of hand and defined numerous conventional objectives without getting some margin to plunk down and craft a quantifiable objective that delivers the specific outcomes we need. That is the reason we need to take those dreams, separate the objectives that all in all make the vision a reality, pick one major one, to begin with, and make it shrewd.

So since you have a couple of major objectives chosen, now is the right time to accomplish the work to go through and ensure they're following the rules of a brilliant objective.

A brilliant objective is one that is

S - Specific

M - Measurable

A - Achievable

R - Relevant

T - Time-bound

As such, they're tight and not unclear, they produce a quantifiable outcome, they're feasible, they're connected with your qualities and they have a set cutoff time.

Compose S.M.A.R.T on a piece of paper and check to ensure your objective is following the standards. Try not to be tempted to skip this step, yet rather adhere to this dependable objective setting technique so you'll remain focused and kill your objectives with certainty.

Be Strong-Minded and Dedicated

Imagine a scenario in which you got up 15 minutes ahead of schedule consistently to zero in on your major objective. Imagine a scenario where you just did one little job a day that will draw you nearer to accomplishing it. Where might you be in about a year?

I realize 15 minutes doesn't seem like a lot, yet it adds up rapidly - an hour and a half a year to be exact. So the "I don't have enough time" excuse basically doesn't cut it any longer. On the off chance that it's fundamentally important, you'll set aside a few minutes.

Sincerely commit to yourself to chip away at the needle-movers in your day-to-day existence, regardless of whether it's something insignificant. Perhaps it's pretty much as straightforward as going through 5 minutes defining your top boundaries for the afternoon or as perplexing as composing your arrangements for the following half year.

Anything that it is, cut out the break of your day to make it happen and if you truly need to remain focused, set cutoff times for yourself with updates on your phone. I believe you should complete every day feeling revived and enabled, not crushed.

Break It Down

You're making these plans, you're laying out your objectives and aims for the year, however when the opportunity arrives to make a move, you hush.

You're deadened by the overpowering of having these immense objectives looming over your head or perhaps you simply don't have any idea where to begin so you shut down. Isn't that so?

Well, the main thing I believe you should do when you feel that uneasiness bubbling up is to take a full breath. Uneasiness will in general make things look way greater than they truly are, so realize that you have one or the other it's not as large of an arrangement as it appears, I guarantee.

Then, you really must separate your bigger assignments into lesser, more reasonable pieces. The key here is to zero in on every little step you want to take, as opposed to view at the higher perspective in general since that is the point at which it gets overpowering.

So after you've defined your Savvy objectives, record the steps you really want to initiate to accomplish them and afterward move them onto your schedule. Give yourself severe cutoff times so you'll be roused to adhere to them.

Honor yourself and your schedule by completely finishing your objectives. Then, at that point, in 12 months' time, you can give yourself a major reviving congratulatory gesture since you achieved all that you set off to do.

Assess and Change

As conditions and circumstances change, so do your arrangements. Assuming you feel like your arrangements are lopsided with where you need to take them, at that point, that is an indication that now is the right time to change them.

Towards the end of every month, I go over my achievements and disappointments, what functioned excellently, what didn't function excellently and what can be improved sometime later. I likewise guarantee that my objectives actually apply to my life dreams, and in the event that not, then, at that point, I make essential changes.

This guarantees that I'm continuously keeping focused on my objectives and I'm not drifting away from the way, meandering into a heading that I never expected to head.

There have been a lot of times that I needed to make turns in my business when I was presently not enthusiastic about my work. I want to say it was simple, yet it was so worth the effort since I serve people much better when I feel good about the thing I'm doing.

The point here is that rolling out an improvement is rarely past the point of no return. It's smarter to face a challenge and change things up than to remain caught where you're hopeless and deadened because that doesn't help anyone.

You serve individuals much better while you're working on your strengths. So if you're not where you have any desire to be, then in my shrewd expressions, "Turn!"

Pick Apart Your Life to Accomplish Your Objectives

When did you realize you needed to be a specialist or the profession you're in?

Whenever that point happened, you began figuring out your existence without knowing it. You began in view of the objective, to be a specialist for instance and you sorted out what steps it would take for you to arrive. Then you went out with tireless energy and drive and got it going or are getting it going. That is the precise exact thing it means to pick apart something, begin considering the objective and basically sort out some way to arrive.

For some of you, that choice was made in secondary school thus you sorted out that you expected to go to a decent school and afterward to clinical school. Obviously, you might've hit a few knocks en route. Perhaps you probably required a little while off to do research to work on your application yet you never removed your eyes from the award.

Do we neglect?

Be that as it may, once the vast majority of us arrive at the promised land, we appear to have failed to remember how picking apart functions. We just let our positions and others direct the way that our lives will wind up. Need to resolve 50 weeks of the year to get 2 weeks free days free? All things considered, I surmise I must choose between limited options.

Work to the bone until we're 65 so we can ideally retire with enough to last the rest of our lives. Certainly, I suppose there could be no alternate way.

You don't have the foggiest idea about the number of specialists that I've heard express the craving to resign early at some time or another or wish for an alternate direction throughout everyday life. Notwithstanding, at whatever point I ask them what they will probably arrive at, they haven't the foggiest idea. For reasons unknown, we've failed to remember how to pick apart our way to our objectives.

Indeed, we realize it will not occur by some coincidence. We additionally realize that the field isn't presumably going in the correct heading to assist you with understanding your optimal life.

So what do we do?

Indeed, it begins by steering genuine positive developments. Here is my straightforward manual for picking apart your life:

1. Begin by sorting out what you maintain that your life should resemble in 5, 10, 20, or 30 years. Think about your profession, family, area, and way of life as you do this. Get it on paper.
2. Sort out whether your ongoing circumstance is probably going to get you to those objectives. Tell the truth. In the event that it is, amazing, you're all set, continue doing what you're doing and quit reading here. In the event that is not, forge ahead and here's where it gets fascinating.
3. This is where you really want to work everything out. What accurate advances and changes do you have to make to get you on the way to your objectives? Perhaps it's an alternate work/position, perhaps making brilliant speculations produce automated revenue to save time, or perhaps it's moving to an alternate state altogether. Get explicit.

Personally, I attempt to do this evaluation no less than two times a year to ensure my eyes are still on the prize.

Understand that this life is the only one you have and it's never too late to make changes

What different things have you been effective in figuring out in your life?

Preferably, you want to have both, a direction and a point of view. With a direction, you know where you're going. With a viewpoint, you know how to arrive. Picking your direction and viewpoint deliberately will support your fulfillment and outcome throughout everyday life. You can utilize the picking apart activity on any objective; however, it is particularly powerful on large, bold life objectives.

The Instinctive Approach to Moving towards Objectives

At the point when we put forth an objective, we do the principal activity step that's the most normal to us. This is the most instinctive thing to do when we put forth an objective that we are energetic about. That is most certainly more powerful than doing nothing. Nonetheless, in the event that we obtain no huge outcomes, we could get demotivated and abandon our objective.

The Viable Approach to Moving towards Objectives

Figuring out is the direct inverse of what falls into place without a hitch for us. In this technique, we don't begin all along, however, we start from the end and we work our direction in reverse. At each step, we pose ourselves the accompanying inquiry.

"What requirements are essential to understand this objective?"

When we find a solution to the inquiry above, we pose a similar inquiry for the response we found. We continue to pose this inquiry until we think of an activity step that can be quickly executed. How about we work on a model where our life objective is financial freedom?

- What requirements are needed to accomplish independence from the rat race?
- My investment funds ought to cover my costs until the end of my life.
- What requirements are needed to develop my investment funds to that level?

- I want to increase my income.
- I want to save routinely a lot of my pay.
- I want to construct an expanded arrangement of ventures.
- What requirements are needed to expand my pay?
- I want to get an advancement or get a superior paying line of work.
- What requirements are needed to get an advancement or to get a superior paying line of work?
- …

Assuming you proceed with the picking apart cycle above, you could concoct the accompanying swift activity steps. As you see, we make three unique objectives in the subsequent step. Assuming you make different objectives at any step, make a point to apply the figuring out interaction to every one of the objectives that you make at any step, so you can arrive at the immediate action step for every one of them.

- Contact the Human Resource Division to decide the range of abilities required for an advancement.
- Save 10% of my pay.

- Spend thirty minutes consistently to study about constructing an enhanced portfolio.

The Impacts of Figuring out at the forefront of Your Thoughts

With figuring out the process, you find your quick activity steps, yet you additionally perceive how your prompt activity steps are associated with your final objective. This holds you back from getting demotivated on the off chance that you obtain no outcomes from your immediate activity steps.

"Working from the ultimate objective in reverse motions gives your deep mind the signal that the objective is now achieved."

Figuring out likewise places you in another frame of mind. Working from the ultimate objective in reverse motions gives your deep mind the signal that the objective is as of now achieved. That keeps your profound brain from concocting a wide range of obstructions. Assuming you start all along and work your way forwards, your profound psyche unwittingly kills the means that are beyond your usual range of familiarity.

Toward the end, you think of a first activity step that is the most agreeable to you, yet all at once not really the best one. With the figuring-out method, you have no good reasons except to find the best step that you can think of. There's no possibility to trick yourself.

The natural approach to moving toward objectives is to begin from where you are and work in your direction towards your objective. At the point when you utilize that methodology, your brain disposes off activities that are beyond your usual range of familiarity and concocts the activities that you know all about.

The successful approach to moving toward objectives is the opposite way around, begin from the end and work your direction back to where you are presently. This signals to your profound psyche that you have proactively accomplished your objective. You let your profound psyche sort out the intelligent strides between your objective and where you are presently. This technique keeps your psyche from disposing off the activity steps that are beyond your usual range of familiarity.

CHAPTER 7

TRANSFORMING OBLITERATION INTO A VALUABLE OPEN DOOR

Catastrophes have an unfortunate underlying meaning as they involve misfortune, passing, interruption, and destruction. We associate them with pictures of obliteration and destruction, of houses covered deep during an avalanche, or frightened individuals shook by a quake. Many individuals consider catastrophes "demonstrations of God" or something unchangeable as far as we might be concerned.

That is where the issue lies. On the off chance that individuals have zero power over debacles, government frontrunners and we most definitely can take off from responsibility. In particular, it removes any chance of progress and gaining from a calamity.

An alternate point of view, some agreement among established researchers focuses on fiascos as anthropogenic. They are man-made. Catastrophes happen when perils connect with weak human exercises and the absence of the ability to endure shocks in the framework. Tropical storms are not really calamities when they happen in the Pacific Sea without prompting any human or monetary misfortunes. They possibly become a calamity when an ill-conceived and overseen seepage framework gets immersed with floodwaters and causes loss of work, injury, or death of individuals. Consequently, a catastrophic event can't exist.

This thought process is significant, on the grounds that it implies that people and their government have an option for them, the ability to forestall or lessen catastrophe chances. Such a point of view intends that there can be valuable open doors following a catastrophe.

History gives more than adequate cases. The Federal Emergency Management Agency was made following the calamities of the 1970s in the US. The idea of Build Back Better arose following the destruction brought about by the 2004 Indian Ocean earthquake and tsunami. In the Philippines, Hurricane "Ondoy" gave areas of strength for the sanctioning of Republic Act No.

10121 or the country's disaster risk reduction and management law.

Building back better, Coronavirus challenges a considerable portion of our suppositions about catastrophes. The nation is oftentimes hit by hurricanes that keep going for a couple of days. This pandemic is different as it unleashes ruin for a really long time. While hurricanes call for critical strategy shifts after a fiasco, this extensive pandemic requires significant arrangement changes to occur during a catastrophe. Leaders with responsive and momentary methodologies moored for the most part on gives are gotten ill-equipped by a pandemic that requires definitive and thoroughly examined strategic choices. To ascribe disappointments in dealing with this emergency to nature or the heavenly turns out to be much more unimportant.

While our nation has fortified its reaction instruments to hydro meteorological and geographical catastrophes, there has been less consideration paid to pandemics. This makes sense of why both the private and public sectors struggled with wrestling with Coronavirus.

A large part of the illustrations from Coronavirus will arise from now on, as pioneers examine its suggestions and more logical investigations arise. Notwithstanding, there are a few examples that can be gathered at this point. To begin with, the nation's regulations and approaches ought to have components to relieve and oversee pandemics. The wellbeing framework assumes a vital part in the public methodology to battle pandemics and merits support in subsidizing hierarchical changes, and Human Resources. Second, alternate courses of action in the confidential area ought to plan for momentary disturbances as well as for the long haul to forestall the deficiency of business of millions of individuals. Third, catastrophe schooling is urgent in making individuals more ready, yet additionally for them to request better authority during fiascos. These illustrations are crucial for the Philippines to incorporate back better frameworks and transform the Coronavirus pandemic into an open door.

For business people, the main constants in business are obstacles, difficulties, turns, and frequently a greater number of disappointments than victories. They face snags the entire day.

From persuading financial backers to give them cash, to battling to meet finance. Managing bombed costly speculations, moving unforeseen complexities, or sending off another item in the market during the unfavorable time, eventually many arrive at the understanding that not all business people are ready to deal with the journey.

The people who make it figure out how to transform the obstacles into clearing their direction to progress. They appear to know how to transform the ceaseless stream of troubles into benefits and arise considerably more grounded and more fruitful.

Dissimilar to the individuals who lose their heads when exposed to such deterrents, making the most of awful times and changing over disappointments and hindrances into open doors is the way into the long existence of any business.

"Poor organizations are obliterated by crises; great organizations endure them; extraordinary organizations are improved by them."

Consider Disappointments to Be Open Doors

Considering development in the midst of disappointment sounds unreasonable, yet it is the best thing you can do to battle disappointment and obliteration in your life. It can flip around disappointment and change a reviled destiny into a favored one.

"Doubling down during difficulties isn't cliché; it's what separates the winners from the wailers."

As a matter of some importance, you need to encounter disappointments to learn and develop. If instead of gaining from disappointments, you feel crushed and quit, the outcomes can be hazardous.

For example, suppose you put resources into a stock that quickly doesn't live up to your assumptions, and you lose a portion of your cash, you have two approaches:

1. Is to discover that maybe "it was not the ideal opportunity to invest in" or you ought to have put resources into a profit development organization, and afterward set this experience to work while organizing the next investment.

2. You feel furious and crushed by the misfortune and quit financial planning.

The first choice is more attractive and valuable, where you turn your failures into an aide for your journey towards progress.

Hindrances or crises in business are really the chance to develop, however just for individuals with boldness to do such. During the season of crises, while generally becoming scared of misfortunes, later on, a sane and sagacious business visionary exploits things like the dropped costs of production, real estate, and unrefined substances. They take advantage of the lower costs of products and transform a crisis into an upper hand.

Pay special attention to open doors inside disappointments, snags, or trouble. It assists with building a positive development mentality.

"A positive attitude will view everything as an open door. With a positive way to deal with a crisis, leaders can settle on better choices with certainty."

This attitude likewise assists with fostering a reassuring workplace for everybody in the organization in light of appreciation, rather than dread. A learned leader with an enthusiastic team converts into an unstoppable business that has one success after the other.

Transforming Disappointments into Open Doors

What are the best tactics to change over a disappointment into an open door? The essential is to think in an unexpected way. Try not to let your impression of occurrences cloud your judgment with "it isn't possible" thinking.

Insist that problems are pliable, not concrete. Have confidence in your capacity to get something going that is by all accounts unthinkable for other people. This methodology of reasoning contrastingly has brought forth giants like Microsoft and LinkedIn in the midst of financial crises.

One more well-known strategy to rise out of disappointment as a victor is to expect the obstacles before they appear. The key is to practice in your brain and on paper what could turn out badly and to which degree, and devise an arrangement to manage it. Utilizing this method, you can keep away from crises and outperform competitors who didn't plan as well as you.

The main thing to remember is that your work isn't to stay away from disappointment or hindrances, they are ensured to occur. Each effective business person will let you know that disappointments occur, challenges occur, it's not how frequently you get wrecked, it's the means by which frequently and how quickly you get back up.

There is a justification for why numerous effective business visionaries were likewise extremely dynamic in sports when more youthful. You need to "be a competitor in mindset" to prevail in business and throughout everyday life.

"Figure out how to see disappointments as effectively demonstrated techniques for what doesn't work, and through the method of elimination, get to the strategy that does."

To get the best out of impediments, you want to consider them to be an amazing chance to gain from. If anything disastrous happens to you, own the disappointment.

Analyze each step of your strategy, your team members' role, and the utilization of assets. Distinguish and pinpoint the reason for disappointment and restart the assignment based on what you have gained from it.

Allow your past obstacles to act as a beacon to cruise through the expanse of hardships. Convert the issues and difficulties you face, into figuring out how to get to your final location of accomplishment.

CHAPTER 8

INFLUENCE LEADERSHIP TO ACHIEVE ANYTHING

How to Best Control Leadership Moments

Frequently when we consider leadership, we ponder those vital instants in history when a famous individual stood before a gathering and gave a viewpoint or a way of thinking that tested our thoughts and inspired us to scrutinize our convictions.

At the point when Winston Churchill said, *"Never give in, never give in, never, never, never, never in nothing, extraordinary or little, huge or frivolous. Never give in except to convictions of honor and good sense,"* he motivated reflection and those paying attention to show more prominent purpose. Over a long time back, Martin Luther King Jr. stood on the steps of the Lincoln Memorial and declared these words: *"I have a dream that my four young kids will one day live in a country where they won't be judged by the shade of their skin but by the substance of their personality."* His words are an enduring suggestion to search internally and perceive that the fundamental part of humankind comes not from our visible presentation, but rather from what our identity is and the way in which we influence that to lift the world.

There are incalculable instances of people whose words have formed organizations, nations, and even society at large. All in all, why should we remain in the shadows of these lights? How might we perhaps expect that we can have an effect that could as significantly shape the world?

Not all discussions are made equivalent. A few discussions will have more noteworthy importance, more noteworthy effect, and more prominent reach. In any case, each discussion holds the possibility to have an effect. The Dalai Lama once said, *"Similarly as waves spread out when a solitary stone is dropped into water, the activities of people can have widespread impacts."*

As leaders, we should understand that our words convey weight. We have the ability to lift individuals or cripple them. Our words can motivate a dream or make an interruption. We can impart boldness or cause dread and self-question. Extraordinary leaders realize that what we express matters for the simple reason that our words become our people's assertions. How we address them generally builds out the manner in which our people address themselves. What makes our discussions significant? What makes our words swell in the mind of another? In particular, could our words at any point truly have a significant effect? The response is, absolutely.

Characterizing Leadership Moments

Extraordinary leaders realize that the way to move individuals in better bearings is about emphatically affecting what they think and accept. Our contemplations and convictions drive our activities and our activities direct our outcomes. Luckily, as a leader, we have no lack of chance to impact. Truth be told, every discussion will offer us no less than one leadership moment.

These are the minutes in the discussion when we can:

- Build up the vision of the group.
- Sustain the way of life of the group.
- Remember somebody's endeavors or achievement.
- Urge an individual to track down an answer for an issue.
- Challenge a restricting point of view.
- Reevaluate a reason and put somebody into a place of possession.
- Draw out the examples gained from a triumph or a misfortune.
- Construct somebody's self-assurance.
- Assist someone with a better comprehension of the "why" behind things.
- Assist them with seeing the circumstances and logical results of what they do.
- Assist them with having a solid sense of security in facing a challenge or taking a stab at a genuinely new thing.

- Let them know how much you have faith in them.

Perceiving Your Leadership Moments

Like some other skill, our capacity to use leadership minutes comes from training. After significant discussions, ask yourself, *"What was the leadership moment in that discussion?"* Start necessitating a couple of moments to rewind the tape to you. At first, you will get your leadership minutes in reflection. However, the more you reflect, the more honed your abilities will turn into. Quite expeditiously, you will find yourself ready to use your leadership minutes in the actual moment.

Moving what individuals come to think and accept about themselves, you will be astonished at the distinction you can observe in individuals. The harsh edges in your most obstinate and negative people could start to mellow. Your group could arrange and team up more. Challenges that recently appeared to be difficult presently don't look so threatening. Your people will start to come to you with ideas and answers rather than simply a clothing rundown of issues. All that will appear to be changed, all due to your words.

Teachings in Leadership: Successful Leveraging

Sales managers experience success when individuals from their sales group experience both group and professional achievement. Managers and sales experts can team up to use every other's assets and make achievements together.

This road map in leadership talks about how collaboration can lead to departmental and individual professional success. In our current reality where assumptions for execution keep on expanding, this assertion contains certifiable worth:

The simplest method for finding true success in the future is together.

Nearly everything of significant worth any individual might achieve in life includes, at some levels, others. Contingent upon the everyday issue you've decided to improve, making progress may be sure to incorporate family, companions, colleagues, or even us your managers. At the point when at least two individuals cooperate to accomplish a shared objective, we call that leveraging.

The delight of accomplishment can really be reduced when we don't permit others to take an interest and help us. Why? Because we have nobody with whom to genuinely share the joy. As individuals, our feeling of achievement really develops further when we know others who care about us have seen well-deserved improvement or achievement. Additionally, they thus experience joy on the grounds that in some little manner they assisted us with accomplishing our objectives. Since they care about us they really determine a specific measure of fulfillment from our triumphs.

A load is more efficiently moved when everybody pulls in a similar direction.

As managers, we request that all employees acknowledge moral obligation regarding the work they produce. We believe that without the individual responsibility of every worker to their work, more elevated levels of efficiency might in all likelihood never be reached. What you might know nothing about is, we don't anticipate that you should venture out this path to more prominent efficiency and accomplishment alone. We might want to help. We win or lose together.

Our prosperity is attached to your prosperity! So it's to our greatest advantage to assist you with your vocation. We know that occasionally you could feel somewhat awkward imparting to the manager what you could feel are your inadequacies. However, what we'd like you to comprehend is we have deficiencies, as well. We'd like you to realize we frequently contact peers, different offices, companions, and, surprisingly, our own bosses for help since we've discovered that objectives are oftentimes more handily achieved with just enough assistance. In the event that there is a test in achieving valid and compelling leveraging, it might emerge in light of the fact that everybody isn't centered around shared objectives or working in a similar direction.

Assuming you reach out for help and meet with resistance, it very well may be the individual you're asking doesn't understand a similar worth you do in your request. The person might be centered around their own necessities, targets, or plans.

Collaboration Creates Energy For Progress.

If we as a whole work together, the probability of shared accomplishment and the success of our personal and business targets become more likely. This idea, when joined with the benefit of developing more grounded relational connections at work, places us all in a substantially more probable position to get more noteworthy fulfillment and accomplishment. These achievements for the most part happen with less pressure and offer more genuine worth to other people. Who knows? You might be the missing connection somebody around you is searching for to best serve their own drives and without you, the individual in question might battle and fall flat.

Shared Responsibility Is The Bond That Binds Effective Groups.

We comprehend that turning out to be independently centered around the task of the moment or the test of the day is so easy. We, as well, at times end up immersed in our own necessities, troubles, and wants. It's human to be worried about yourself and those nearest to you first. But, it's just when you step outside yourself and permit your endeavors to be joined with the endeavors of others that you start to accomplish more noteworthy outcomes. Like the numerous singular strands of a rope, which pull the heaviness of weight all the more effectively, or the fingers that work in participation and congruity with the hand to get a grip on any item, so the group works best together to achieve any objective.

"TEAM: Together Everybody Achieves More"

Our capacity to work all the more intimately with you to get our shared accomplishments can be improved by you. We accept you have extraordinary potential but numerous people who have had potential have missed the mark regarding their ability since they decided to remain solitary. Should you desire to improve your life as opposed to confusing it, we can offer help. At the point when you pick the help of the managers and the group and afterward in kind proposition your help to other people, you start to rapidly understand the force of leveraging very quickly.

Cooperative energy: the combined sum is better than its parts.

At the point when at least two things, individuals, or associations cooperate, the outcome is frequently more prominent than the number of their individual impacts or abilities. This is cooperative energy.

This idea ought to move every one of us to cooperate to accomplish a common good. The common good can be the common obligation to and the accomplishment of individual, group, interdepartmental, and organization goals. One of the reliable side-effects of holding this sort of shared responsibility is a more useful, cheerful, and satisfying workplace.

The main concern is, your occupation really gets more straightforward when you help other people and permit others to help you

Legacy Intensive Leadership

Legacy leadership has an approach to making leaders stop and reflect. Now and again those reflections are brought into the world from the conditions of what we see and experience around us right now.

These reflections produce either a feeling of certification that everything is great, or that something needs to change; that the current circumstance can be better.

Leaders Keeping Goals

During circumstances in the present, we direct our concentration toward the future and what could be. Many fresh new goals are a result of this sort of reflection.

Legacy Leadership Pulls Attention to the Past

We review the great time encounters and connections. A portion of these reflections bring mindfulness that errors have been made, or things have become motionless. Different circumstances can deliver recollections of the past.

Funerals and other remembrances are genuine instances of these kinds of reflections. A new family memorial service was a sweet season of recollecting the many encounters of a caring grandmother as well as a grandfather who passed away ten years ago. This was additionally a consolation to respect them, by proceeding with the practices and feelings that they demonstrated.

The Human Condition Is Driven To Make Some Meaningful Difference

Independently or on the whole, we make progress toward the prizes and titles. Establishing and praising standards and accomplishments. In the postmodern, individual-driven world we live in today, the craving to leave a heritage is too often egotistical.

John F. Kennedy has said, *"The reasonable beneficiary takes cautious inventory of his legacies and gives a devoted accounting to those whom he owes a commitment of trust."* This opinion addresses the relationship we all have with each other.

Legacy Leadership

According to a leadership viewpoint, this is a significant point. Legacy leadership expands what may frequently, erroneously, be perceived as an individual and solitary activity.

While the underlying impetus for authority might begin with the drive of an individual, legacy leadership must be accomplished when leaders develop other leaders.

This improvement doesn't occur in a vacuum. It occurs locally.

Shrewd leaders remember they are important part of a history of authority (positive or negative) that they have come into themselves, impacted in the present, and will shape how those that follow them will lead into the future.

CONCLUSION
Making the Most of It and Carrying On With a Decent Life

Enjoying a quality lifestyle can mean something else for everybody. Notwithstanding, there is as yet a general comprehension of what this thought involves to most people living in the modern world. The good life, in its most basic structure, is a progression of endless fulfillment that just develops as time goes on.

The good life comprises of wanting to get up each day, eager to take on anything that each day has in store for you. It doesn't have anything to do with the material belongings or misleadingly incited sensations. The good life depends on the sympathetic deeds you play out, the individual objectives you endeavor to accomplish, and the legacy you choose to leave behind because of the imprint you made on your general surroundings.

You won't ever make the most of your life until you fill your heart with joy. You won't ever fill your heart with joy until you make the most of each and every hour. You won't ever make the most of each and every hour until you make the most of each and every second. You won't ever make the most of each and every second until you make the most of your actions. You won't ever make the most of your actions until you make the most of your words. You won't ever make the most of your words until you make the most of your thoughts.

Life counts when you know that every day is a countdown to your departure from earth. Life counts when you go with a choice to make the most of it. Your choices can never count until you have the discipline to make the most of them. Achievement is a propensity you embrace consistently and the earlier you get into that mindset, the sooner you will actually want to bring forth prospects you probably won't have envisioned

Along these lines, until your propensities count, your life can't count. How about we unwind the fruitful propensities that should be drilled day to day for life to count?

Your predetermination rises or falls as indicated by the measure of your life demeanor. Until you create and keep up with positive life perspectives day to day, life goes down into the channel of the drains of average quality. The mentality is a key course in the school of progress. Positive daily routine mentalities is the doorway to effective living and it comprises; the manner in which you see yourself; the manner in which you see and relate with others; and your point of view.

Satisfaction is an obligation that can't be designated. Pondering about yourself and your capacities; thinking and acting decidedly towards others; talking emphatically in your discussions and being around positive individuals will cause your life to float towards the area of accomplishment. The utilization of your time decides the usefulness of your life. The value you attach to time decides the value you will make throughout everyday life.

Effective individuals focus on their life; they plan their day cautiously and totally finish their arrangements. Life counts when you work on the establishment in light of the General Law of Significance which states:

"Do not squander your energy on thoughts, individuals, or actions which are not worthy. Do not squander your thoughts on ideas that are not worthy. Do not squander your energy on events that are not worthy. Do not squander your cash on that which isn't cash".

In this way, focusing on your life consistently in the radiance of your vision will lift you from the shores of inability to the mountain ridge of progress. As the saying goes, *"health is wealth"* is indisputable. We all want to find success, however, not to the detriment of our wellbeing. Remaining sound is a resource that should be kept up with through appropriate sustenance and dietary pattern, workout, cheerful attitude, rest, and the capacity to actually deal with pressure. Consequently, a positive way of life that promotes great well-being ought to be developed.

One of the significant propensities that ensure a good outcome is responsibility. Your everyday choice to remain committed put you aside from the half-doers in the game of life; the people who never finish what they start and who trust that every one of the circumstances will be wonderful before they start to have their impact on the phase of life. Keep in mind, life will test how committed you are prior to giving up to you its vault of resources. Accordingly, consider the consequences; decide to follow through on the cost; take a stab at greatness; keep up with your concentration, and be focused; no retreat till the star inside you arises.

Your life can never count until you are esteem driven as opposed to swarm driven. What do you rely on? Is it true or not that you are being cleared by the flow of individuals' perspectives and activities or do you stem the tide by deciding to *"stick out"* in any event, when *"everyone blends in"*? Creating positive qualities and living it out consistently give you a strong starting point for your fate to be based on and furthermore supports it from destruction. Development is a word that is essential in the vocabulary of progress. Self-awareness includes working on oneself; profoundly, intellectually; socially;

sincerely, and monetarily. Have a self-awareness plan; read books that will redesign you; go to classes, and preparation phases; look for and assemble every great information that is accessible to you to work on your life. Be a consistent student in the space of life.

Your life can never count on the off chance that you don't enhance others' life. In the space of accomplishment; effective relationships is key. Put a high worth on individuals; regard and care for them.

www.ingramcontent.com/pod-product-compliance
Lightning Source LLC
Chambersburg PA
CBHW050006230526
45465CB00003BB/1290